W9-DBW-765

Everything the

Instructors Never Told You

About Mogul Skiing

Dan DiPiro

authorHOUSE™

1663 LIBERTY DRIVE, SUITE 200
BLOOMINGTON, INDIANA 47403
(800) 839-8640
WWW.AUTHORHOUSE.COM

© 2005 Dan DiPiro. All Rights Reserved.

No part of this book may be reproduced, stored in a retrieval system, or transmitted by any means without the written permission of the author.

First published by AuthorHouse 08/25/05

ISBN: 1-4208-6159-X (sc)

Library of Congress Registration Number: TXu 1-226-856

Printed in the United States of America
Bloomington, Indiana

This book is printed on acid-free paper.

All photographs by John McNamara (john@picturesrhodeisland.com).

Design and layout by Emily DiPiro (dipirodesign@cox.net).

Inquiries and author correspondence should be sent via e-mail to Marketing and Publicity Manager Kim Stone (kim@free-lancewriter.com).

For more information about this book, visit www.learnmoguls.com.

For my parents, who gave me the opportunities to
discover both skiing and writing;
and for my wife, who accompanies me through
all the bumps and icy troughs.

Author's Acknowledgements

For encouraging me throughout the writing, editing and production of this book, I gratefully thank my wife, Kenna. Many thanks to my friend, award-winning travel and ski writer and editor Jonathan D. Auerbach, for the editing work he contributed to the project. Thanks to John McNamara for his great ski photography and for the fun we had shooting it. And many thanks to my sister Emily DiPiro, for providing the book with its beautiful design and layout.

CONTENTS

INTRODUCTION

Why are so many fit, expert skiers baffled by the moguls? And why is useful mogul-skiing advice so hard to find?

Most skiers don't realize that mogul skiing requires a special set of techniques that have nothing to do with groomed-trail skiing. Most skiers try to simply carry their groomed-trail techniques into the moguls. With no knowledge of mogul techniques, these skiers are bound to struggle in the bumps.

Outside of competitive mogul-skiing circles (competitors, former competitors, coaches, judges, devotees, etc.) mogul techniques remain largely unknown and unaddressed. Most ski instructors teach only groomed-trail techniques (techniques derived from alpine racing) and aren't even familiar with the special techniques used by mogul skiers. Yes, most ski schools do offer mogul-skiing lessons, but many of these lessons are ineffective, because they encourage students to use only groomed-trail techniques in the bumps. From such a lesson, a student can hope to learn no more than a mean- dering, wide-stance style of skiing that will vastly limit her mogul-skiing potential. Such lessons are more about mogul *survival* than mogul skiing.

Most of the written mogul-skiing advice one finds in maga- zines and books, and on Web pages, is just as inadequate as the average on-snow mogul lesson. Most of this advice is produced by ski-instruction writers who, like their on-snow counterparts, don't know mogul technique. And in the rare instances where good mogul skiers have authored a bit of authentic advice, that advice has been so small a snippet of the whole picture that it has left its readers with only more questions.

With little to no knowledge of mogul technique, many would-be bump enthusiasts have simply thrown up their hands and surrendered. After repeated failures in the bumps, these otherwise capable skiers have told themselves that mogul skiing must lie beyond the reach of the average expert skier, that it must be for daredevils only. And this daredevil myth has grown and pushed the downhill skiing masses even further from the pleasures and thrills of mogul skiing.

Skiing moguls is not about daredevilry. It's not about taking unreasonable chances. It's not about closing your eyes, hoping for the best, and just going for it. Skiing moguls well is about physical fitness, practice and proper technique. With the right technique, most fit, expert skiers can become good mogul skiers. And some can become great mogul skiers, and even great competitors.

Under the guidance of freestyle coaches, children on free-style teams all over the world are learning mogul techniques and skiing moguls well. I've successfully taught mogul tech-niques to skiers as young as 11 and as old as 60. I know, from my own teaching experiences, that most fit, expert skiers who want to ski bumps can learn to ski bumps.

Whether you want to ski gentle moguls with comfort and confidence, turn heads on your local mogul run, or compete in mogul contests, this book will give you the specialized knowledge you need to reach your goal. If you practice the techniques I describe in this book, you'll gradually gain more and more comfort, confidence and ability in the bumps. You won't need to take any huge, dangerous leaps. You won't need to take big chances with your physical safety. You'll just steadily get better, as you would were you practicing tennis or golf or any other sport. With practice, you'll be doing things in the moguls that you once thought you could never do.

Some of the techniques I describe in this book are similar to well-known groomed-trail techniques. In some cases, the difference between the mogul technique and the corresponding groomed-trail technique is subtle. But these subtle differences are crucial. All of the techniques I describe in this book are vital to good mogul skiing. They are techniques that have proven their worth in the demanding, put-up-or-shut-up realm of competitive bump skiing. They are techniques that work well in the bumps, whether you ski bumps at five miles-per-hour or 30 miles-per-hour. They are the techniques you must add to your groomed-trail skills, if you're going to become a mogul skier or a true all-mountain expert. They are techniques that produce a style of downhill skiing that is appreciably different from the skiing styles of most instructors and racers. And they are techniques of which a surprisingly large number of instructors, ski-instruction writers and racers are remarkably unaware.*

Dan DiPiro
Easton, New Hampshire
Summer, 2005

* I use the word "technique" in the way that the larger, English-speaking world uses the word, not in the way that most ski instructors use it. Some instructors might argue that what I call "techniques" are actually "tactics." With the technique/tactic argument, instructors will downplay the significant technical differences between mogul skiing and groomed-trail skiing, and suggest that there are only minor "tactical" differences between the two. I strongly disagree with this suggestion and believe that it has prevented good skiers from learning authentic mogul skills. Aspiring bump skiers need to understand that the moguls require significantly different ways of doing things, that the moguls require some significantly different techniques.

1. SOME GENERAL ADVICE

Before you practice any of the drills in this book, read at least the first seven chapters of the book in their entirety. For the sake of clarity and organization, I've described a distinct set of techniques with each chapter. In practice, however, these techniques are not so distinct. On the snow, they work together. Before you practice any single mogul technique, therefore, gain a complete overview of mogul skiing.

With everything, start small, then work your way up. Several of the chapters in this book include drills for you to practice on groomed terrain. Don't skip these drills. And when you begin to practice a skill in the bumps, start with just a few bumps on a gentle slope that runs onto groomed snow. You should also practice on small bumps; this is the safest and most effective way to learn mogul skiing. Ski small bumps, then medium size bumps, then larger bumps. Become a mogul skier first on gentle moguls, then step it up to the big, steep stuff, if that's what you want to do.

Before you try any other mogul technique, master the "home" mogul-skiing posture on groomed terrain. If you're already a groomed-trail expert, learning the home posture may take you just a few runs. If you're not an expert, learning the home posture will probably take you a while longer. Don't ski challenging moguls until after you've mastered the home posture on groomed terrain.

You should also know that not every skier is destined to ski steep bump trails at 30 miles per hour. If you are, this book will help you get there. If you aren't, this book can help you reach a more modest goal: say, skiing the fall line on a somewhat bumpy, intermediate trail, and doing it with the smoothness, efficiency, control and style of a real bump skier.

Finally, a few words about safety. Mogul skiing, like other forms of downhill skiing, can cause injuries. While you don't need to be a daredevil to become a good mogul skier, you might be more likely to hurt yourself while skiing moguls than while slowly cruising a groomed trail. If you come to the sport in good physical fitness, however, and if you use the right techniques, you'll greatly reduce your chances of injuring yourself.

In several ways, mogul skiing is actually much safer than most people think it is. For example, when you ski moguls with the proper absorption and extension techniques, the impact the bumps deliver to your knees and back is often not as hard as the impact delivered by a jog on a hard road. Secondly, while high-speed lifts have overpopulated many ski areas and thereby made collisions with other skiers and riders more common on groomed, high-speed thoroughfares, collisions remain relatively uncommon on mogul trails. And, obviously, if you're the sort of groomed-trail skier who makes a lot of high-speed turns near the woods, mogul skiing is a comparatively safer form of skiing for you... and the trees.

2.   YOUR HOME POSTURE

Alpine racers and other groomed-trail devotees tend to crouch. That is, they tend to ski with a relatively large amount of bend in their backs and legs. While crouching can have its advantages on the race course and elsewhere on groomed trails, it doesn't work well in the moguls.

Many skiers crouch on the mogul field because they've grown accustomed to crouching on groomed trails. Some skiers have also grown accustomed to crouching while playing other sports; shortstops, tennis players and all sorts of other athletes crouch to ready themselves for play. Skiers also tend to crouch in the bumps because bumps present the skier with adversity, and crouching is a natural, defensive reaction to adversity. We tend to feel safer, more stable, more prepared, when we're closer to the ground.

In the moguls, however, crouching limits your ability to absorb bumps. When you can't absorb bumps well, you're likely to lose your balance and your speed-control. Crouching in the moguls also causes back and neck strain, and generally compromises your strength. To ski well, the bumper must ski with a relatively upright torso, and relatively extended legs.

The Drill: Stand tall

Stand on a groomed, intermediate trail with your skis pointed across the hill (perpendicular to the fall line), so that you don't slide away. Now stand up tall on your skis by straight-ening your legs and torso. From your feet to your head, your body should form a relatively straight line that's perpendicular to your skis. Now flex your hips, knees and ankles slightly. When you do this, your hips will drop an inch or two closer to the snow. Don't, however, allow your hips to drop too far back over your heels or the tails of your skis. Your weight should be centered enough over your skis so that your shins are pressed against the tongues of your boots. Your torso should be rela-tively upright, not bent forward. (To put it another way: your chest should not be dropped down towards the snow.) And your legs should be relatively extended, not too deeply flexed.

Now let's put this posture into motion. Ski the groomed, intermediate run on which you're standing, and try to maintain

Aspiring bump skiers should first master the tall "home" mogul-skiing posture on groomed ter-rain.

this tall posture as you ski. If, while you ski, you feel yourself crouching, stand up tall again by extending your legs and returning your torso to the upright position. Think of moving your hips up (skyward) and forward (down the hill). This will keep you from crouching and leaning back. Be sure to maintain that shin-to-tongue pressure all the way down the hill.

Repeat this drill on groomed, intermediate terrain until you feel comfortable with this relatively tall posture, and you're able to maintain it throughout all of your groomed-trail runs.

In the bumps, it's home

Once you've mastered this tall posture on a groomed trail, you'll be trying it in gentle moguls. Chapter 4 will describe the extension technique that will allow you to bring this tall posture into the moguls.

This mogul-skiing posture is your "home" posture, not your constant posture. That is, it's the posture with which you will begin your mogul run, and the posture to which you will immediately return after you absorb each bump. In order to absorb each mogul, you'll need to bend at the hips, knees and ankles (only minimally at the back). As you pass each mogul, however, you'll quickly return to your tall home posture so that you're prepared to absorb the next mogul. Again, this "return to home" works hand-in-hand with the extension technique described in Chapter 4.

Your home posture is the tall posture with which you will begin your mogul run, and the posture to which you will immediately return after you absorb each bump.

You may find that using this tall home posture in the bumps is, at first, difficult. Moguls look scarier than groomed terrain, so we're more tempted to crouch in defense when confronted with moguls. You'll probably feel this when you first try to assume the home posture in moguls; you'll feel yourself crouching down toward the snow. You'll then need to push your hips up (skyward) and drive them forward (down the hill) to regain your tall home posture. In the bumps, standing up tall and driving your hips down the hill can be frightening. Once you get the feel for your home posture, however, you'll come to know and understand its advantages, and you'll grow increasingly comfortable with it. But let's look more closely at those advantages.

Greater ability to absorb bumps and stay centered

Your home mogul-skiing posture gives you a greater range of motion for the absorption of moguls. When you assume your tall home posture – with your legs relatively extended – your legs are like the long front shock absorbers of a dirt bike: they have a lot of potential travel for the absorption of moguls. To put it another way: when you assume your home posture, your legs have a lot of "bend" left in reserve for the absorption of bumps.

When you ski moguls in a crouched position, you don't have much travel or bend left in your legs for mogul absorption. With only limited ability to absorb bumps, you have only limited ability to ski smoothly and keep yourself out of the back seat. And how important is it to keep yourself out of the back seat while you ski moguls? It's absolutely vital.

Skis are designed to perform best when the skier's weight is centered over the ski. When you ski with your weight back over

When you limit your ability to absorb bumps, you limit your ability to maintain balance and control speed.

your heels or ski tails, your skis don't operate correctly. The ski tails lock up in the snow and the skis all but refuse to turn, control speed, and absorb the impact of moguls. When this happens, you quickly gain unmanageable amounts of speed and you're forced to leave the fall line and traverse the trail to regain control.

If you keep your weight distributed evenly along the whole length of the ski (your maintaining that shin-to-tongue pressure indicates that your weight is not too far back), your skis will respond beautifully in the moguls and everywhere else on the mountain. They'll turn when you ask them to turn, stop when you ask them to stop, and help to absorb the impact of moguls.

Minimal back and neck strain

You've probably heard that it's safest to lift heavy objects with your leg muscles rather than your back muscles. In other words, when you bend over to pick up a heavy box or a piece of furniture, you should bend at the ankles, knees and hips, but not so much at the back. This is because your leg muscles are much stronger than your back muscles and much less likely to be strained. In a sense, skiing bumps is like lifting heavy objects; you should do the work with your powerful leg muscles, not your relatively weak back muscles.

Skiing bumps with a relatively upright torso allows you to do most of the work with your leg muscles. When you crouch, your back is put into a near-horizontal position. When you ski into a bump with your back in a near-horizontal position, your head and torso jerk down and forward and your back and neck muscles are forced to absorb much of the impact. With your torso in an upright, near-vertical position, you eliminate a lot of this back and neck strain, because you absorb most of the impact with your powerful leg muscles, rather than your relatively weak back muscles.

Greater overall strength

Because a taller body is a stronger body, your tall, home mogul-skiing posture also gives you more useable muscle strength than you'd have in a crouched position. When you stand tall, with a relatively upright torso and relatively extended legs, you reduce the strain on your muscles by supporting yourself primarily with your skeleton. By reducing positional strain on your muscles – particularly your quadriceps – you give yourself more useable muscle strength, which you can use for absorbing bumps and turning your skis.

3.   ROTARY-POWERED TURNS

To turn their skis, mogul skiers use more rotary force (twisting force, steering) than racers and other groomed-trail devotees tend to use. This additional rotary force has three important benefits in the bumps: firstly, it turns the skis quickly; secondly, it allows the bumper to execute turns while traveling down a relatively narrow corridor of snow; thirdly, it allows the bumper to turn his skis without a lot of constant ski-to-snow contact.

The purely carved turn takes a relatively long time to execute. It takes a long time to tilt the skis on edge, to wait for them to bend, and to then ride those bent skis through the turn (around one gate and toward the next, in the case of the alpine racer). Because moguls are positioned so closely together,* and because the mogul skier must turn his skis with each and every bump in the fall line in order to maintain control of his speed, he has only a brief span of time to execute each turn. This brief span of time demands the quickness of a rotary-powered turn.

Because they are relatively round, carved turns are also relatively wide, and so their execution requires a relatively wide corridor of snow (Illustration B). But mogul skiing is all about moving the torso straight down the fall line while turning the skis within a relatively narrow corridor of snow (Illustration A).

*You'd never see gates placed so closely together on a race course.

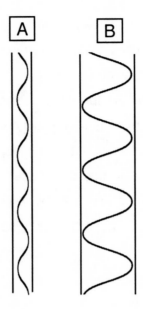

This narrow corridor does not accommodate wide turns. Because the rotary-powered turn does not necessarily move the skier or the skis far across the trail (left-to-right or right-to-left), it can be easily executed within this narrow corridor. To put all of this another way: rotary-powered turns are a good fit for the bumps, width-wise.

Finally, in order to execute a true carved turn, you need a good amount of constant, ski-to-snow contact like that which you enjoy on a groomed trail. In the dramatically undulating mogul fall line, your skis enjoy less constant, ski-to-snow contact (especially when you're skiing quickly through big moguls), which makes true carving in the mogul fall line difficult, if not impossible. The rotary-powered turn, however, can be executed with no snow contact at all: it's possible to steer your skis while they're completely airborne. For this reason, too, the mogul skier uses more rotary force in the turn than the typical groomed-trail devotee.

If you're a devoted disciple of the traditional carved turn and now want to ski moguls well, you'll need to abandon any prejudice you may have about heavy steering. Regardless of what you may hear or read elsewhere, the correct mogul-skiing turn, even as it is executed by the best mogul skiers in the world, is characterized by a relatively large amount of rotary force.

Balance, timing

Keeping your weight centered over your skis is a key to fast, steered turns in the bumps. If you can maintain shin-to-tongue pressure throughout your descent (again, this indicates that your weight is not too far back), your skis will steer easily for you and you'll be able to make smooth, rapid-fire turns.

In the bumps, most skiers lean back over the tails of their skis, which locks up the tails in the snow. When you lean back in the bumps, steering your skis feels like steering an aircraft carrier: it takes ages for things to come around. But when your weight is centered over your skis, steering them from one direction to the other requires very little time or effort. It feels like nothing more than a quick flick of your ski tips.

But there's also a certain amount of timing involved. As you pass a mogul and enter the trough, the snow surface drops away from you, and your skis become, for a moment, less heavily weighted. Or, if you're skiing moguls quickly, your skis may become completely un-weighted (airborne) as you pass the mogul. During these moments when your skis are less heavily weighted, quickly steering them from one direction to the other is easy.

People sometimes talk about the fast feet of mogul skiers as if you have to be born with some rare gift – some special, fast-twitch musculature – to make fast, mogul-style turns. The truth is, if you can keep yourself out of the back seat and initiate your turns when your skis are less heavily weighted, you, too, will have fast feet in the moguls. (I have fast feet in the moguls, but I've never had especially fast feet in any other sport I've played.) When you get your balance and timing right, making fast turns in the moguls is hardly more difficult than steering your skis left and right while you sit on a chairlift with your skis dangling in the air.

A firm edge set at the bump

When you ski through a race course, or carve or "arc" turns down any groomed trail, your torso moves laterally – left-to-right and right-to-left – back and forth across the fall line, as you descend the trail.

When a mogul skier moves through the moguls, however, her torso makes little to no lateral movement; the mogul skier's torso travels in a relatively straight line down the hill.

(Fast mogul skiing feels, to an extent, like falling straight down the hill.) With each turn, however, the mogul skier moves her feet laterally, back and forth across the fall line, beneath her straight-lining torso. Although this lateral motion is relatively subtle, it's enough to end each of her turns with a firm and effective edge set at the bump. This firm edge set at the bump is the part of the turn that most controls the mogul skier's speed, **and she accomplishes it without a lot of racer-like leg or hip angulation.** The firm edge set happens naturally, automatically, when the turned skis meet the uphill face of the bump.

There's a sense in which mogul skiing has more in common with walking down a staircase than with carving turns down a groomed trail. Just as you don't need to dig the edge of your shoe into each step to control your descent down a staircase, you don't need to dramatically angle your skis to gain purchase on the uphill face of a mogul. This is why mogul skiers are able to control speed while skiing with a relatively tall posture and narrow stance, and on a relatively "flat" (not-so-heavily edged) ski. And this is also one of the ways in which mogul skiing differs so substantially from groomed-trail skiing.

When you ski down a groomed trail, the snow surface ahead is nearly always falling away from you. In the moguls, however, the snow surface faces you, faces uphill, at each bump, like a stair tread. These two downhill-skiing surfaces

– the mogul field and the groomed trail – could hardly be more different from one another, and could hardly place more different demands on the skier. It should come as no surprise to anyone, therefore, that mogul skiing requires special techniques that have nothing to do with groomed-trail skiing.

Do mogul skiers skid their turns?

In the minds of most groomed-trail experts, a turn powered by extra rotary force is an impure turn that involves a lot of inefficient skidding. So, with all my talk of rotary motion, am I saying that mogul skiers have a lot of inefficient skidding in their turns? Well, sometimes bumpers skid, and sometimes they don't skid. But the so-called inefficiency of skidding is irrelevant to mogul skiing. The question is akin to asking if a bicycle gets good gas mileage.

In tight, rhythmic moguls, good mogul skiers will sometimes make turns with little to no skidding. They'll execute their rotary movements while their skis are in the air, rebounding laterally across the fall line from one bump to the next, and so the skis don't actually skid on the snow. When the skis contact the snow, they do so with an authoritative edge set at the bump (no skidding), and the skier doesn't release that firm edge set until the skis are back in the air, moving across the fall line again toward the next firm edge set.

But even top mogul competitors will sometimes skid a bit in the middle of the turn, before the edge set at the bump. In moguls that demand more ski-to-snow contact – a steeper slope, for example, with more space between bumps – bump skiers are more likely to perform their rotary motion while their skis are in contact with the snow, which results in a somewhat skidded turn. For the mogul skier, however, a bit of skidding in the turn is not inefficient.*

Alpine racing's carving-versus-skidding standard of turning excellence simply does not apply to mogul skiing. Skidding is inefficient on a race course, where the racer needs to quickly and repeatedly travel far across the fall line, left and right, back and forth, to reach all of the gates around which he must ski. For the racer, a skidded turn is an inefficient means of traversing the hill: it sacrifices too much speed and doesn't efficiently direct the skier across the fall line. This is the main reason for the groomed-trail devotee's valuing the carved turn: the carved turn directs the skier across the hill without wasting much speed.

But the mogul skier does not need or want to ski across the hill! He wants to move his torso straight down the hill. He is concerned with speed control, but not so much with direction control. He pretty much travels in the straight direction in which gravity pulls him, and so he has no need for an efficient means of traversing the fall line. For this reason, the so-called inefficiency of the skidded turn is irrelevant to mogul skiing.

Of course, groomed-trail devotees also value the carved turn because it's a fun way to ski on groomed snow. It's fun to

*In fact, the opposite is true: an overdependence on carving leads to inefficiencies in the bumps.

drop your hip towards the snow and pit centrifugal and gravita-
tional forces against one another as you speed across the fall
line. Like driving through sharp turns in a sports car that hugs
the road, carving and "arcing" turns on skis is a thrill. While
mogul skiing doesn't deliver this particular, turn-carving thrill,
it does deliver a different thrill: the thrill of skiing straight down
a bumpy trail, quickly and smoothly, over and through every
formidable obstacle in your path. This is the thrill that makes
mogul devotees devoted.

Why do bump skiers sometimes talk about carving in the bumps?

Occasionally, a mogul skier or a freestyle coach will talk
or write about carving or "partial carving" in the moguls. Make
no mistake about this. Even world-class mogul turns are characterized by relatively heavy doses of rotary motion: far more
rotary motion than you're used to, if you're used to true carving
and "arcing" on groomed terrain. If you don't believe me, just
watch an Olympic mogul run in slow motion on your VCR.
You'll see the world-class bumper execute the better part of
his turn while his skis are off the snow, in the air, over the
trough. Of course, the only sort of turning one can do in mid
air is pure rotary motion. Manufacturers are yet to invent a ski
that can engage its edge and carve in mid air.

Expert bumpers occasionally call their mogul-style turns
"carving" or "partial carving" for two reasons. Firstly, expert
bumpers do edge very effectively at the bump, at the end of

each turn. Secondly, they allow themselves a very relaxed definition of the word "carve," because they know that if they use this word, the expert skiing masses, which are predominantly comprised of those trained in a racing or racing-derived tradition, will be more likely to respect what bumpers have to say. Groomed-trail experts unfamiliar with mogul technique are always eager to hear mogul skiing described in terms of carving: the turning technique those experts understand and most revere. But all this talk of carving is unfortunate for the aspiring mogul skier who is trying to learn the fundamentals and is led to believe that mogul skiing and pure carving have a lot to do with one another. They don't.

Mogul turning tips

❋ *Stay out of the back seat! (Maintain that shin-to-tongue pressure.)*

❋ *Try pressing your ski tips down onto the snow as you execute each turn.*

❋ *Each of your mogul turns will naturally end with a firm edge set somewhere on, or partly on, the uphill face of the bump. This edge set is the part of your turn that most helps you to control your speed.*

❋ *If you can, get yourself a pair of mogul skis, which are designed for smooth, quick, mogul-style turns. (More about skis in chapter 10.)*

Drill 1: Side slips / pivot slips

Practice side slipping down a groomed intermediate slope. Slide straight down the fall line; don't move right or left as you descend. It may help to imagine that you're moving down a straight corridor about the width of a grocery store aisle. As you side slip, maintain your tall home posture and face your torso down the fall line as much as possible. (A line drawn from shoulder to shoulder would remain nearly perpendicular to the fall line.)

Practice side slipping with your left ski on the downhill side, then with your right ski on the downhill side. Without stopping your descent, switch from one side to the other by rotating your skis through a pivot slip (flatten your skis

The side-slip / pivot-slip drill will accustom you to the feeling of flattening your skis, releasing your edges, and using rotary force to turn the skis, all while you travel straight down the fall line.

on the snow, apply rotary force). Repeat these pivot slips. Remember to stay in the fall line, stay in that narrow corridor, as you descend.

This drill will accustom you to the feeling of flattening your skis, releasing your edges, and using rotary force to turn the skis, all while you travel straight down the fall line. If you've spent most of your skiing life trying to carve or "arc" turns back and forth across the fall line, these slippery, rotary-powered turns and this straight-ahead movement may take some getting used to.

Drill 2: Quick-turn drill

On a groomed, intermediate slope, pick a landmark to which you'll ski. The landmark might be a work road or a bend in the trail or anything at all, and it should be 50 or so yards away. Ski slowly towards the landmark. Your torso should move straight down the fall line as it does during mogul skiing. Make as many quick, rotary-powered turns as you can make before reaching your landmark. These turns will be quick, sliding turns that end with a firm edge set and an energetic rebound into the next turn. They're not carved turns. As you initiate each turn, think of pressing your ski tips down onto the snow. You might also try lifting your heels or ski tails a bit with the start of each turn.

Your goals are to turn your skis from one direction to the other as quickly as possible, to maintain speed control, and to keep your torso moving straight down the fall line. Count the number of turns you're able to make before reaching your

Aspiring bump skiers should first learn and practice the quick, mogul-style turn on groomed terrain.

landmark. When you repeat the run, start in the same place and ski to the same landmark. Try to increase your number of turns with each run.

Don't be discouraged if your feet feel slow on the flats (groomed terrain). It's tougher to steer a quick turn on the flats because your skis are more constantly weighted than they are in the moguls. In the moguls, you'll be able to take advantage of those moments, between bumps, when the snow drops away from you, your skis become light, and you can quickly and easily steer them from one direction to the other.

If you practice this drill regularly on groomed terrain, you'll develop the ability to quickly steer your skis with rotary force, and to maintain speed control with a quick edge set at the end of each turn, all while moving your torso straight down the fall line. Then you'll be able to carry these skills into the moguls.

In the moguls, you'll be able to take advantage of those moments, between bumps, when the snow drops away from you, your skis become light, and you can quickly and easily steer them from one direction to the other.

Not as important as you might think

But don't let all this talk of turns mislead you. While turning is one way the mogul skier controls speed and maintains balance, and while lots of neat, fast, fluid turns earn big points in mogul competition, turning is, in a way, not as crucial for the mogul skier as it is for the groomed-trail skier. On groomed trails, the turn is all-important. It's the skier's sole means of control. In the bumps, however, the turn is just one of two vital means of control. For the bump skier, turns are no more important, and sometimes less important, than absorption and extension.

4. ABSORPTION AND EXTENSION

There's a whole dimension of movement that's nearly exclusive to mogul skiing, a dimension of movement about which groomed-trail devotees hardly ever talk. Groomed trails are, relatively speaking, two-dimensional planes. On these two-dimensional planes, skiers concern themselves, for the most part, with two things: turns to the left, and turns to the right. A mogul field, however, is a three-dimensional beast.

Yes, the bump-skier concerns himself with the left-and-right dimension. But he also concerns himself with the up-and-down dimension. One moment, the bump skier's legs are extended (skis in the trough, home position). The next moment his legs are deeply bent (skis somewhere on the mogul). In bump skiing, absorbing bumps and extending your legs between

Absorbing and extending at a relatively slow speed, in relatively small moguls.

bumps are both absolutely crucial. You cannot ski moguls well without active, well-timed absorption and extension movements.

Absorption and extension serve two important functions in mogul skiing: firstly, they keep the bumps from knocking you around and throwing you off balance; secondly, they help to control your speed.

Absorption and extension are, by the way, the mogul techniques that lie furthest from alpine-racing techniques, and that most differentiate mogul skiing from groomed-trail skiing. The groomed-trail experts who are most baffled by the moguls tend to be those skiers with the poorest understanding of absorption and extension.

A quiet upper body

Absorption and extension keep the bumps from knocking you around and throwing you off balance. To put this into mogul skiers' terms: absorption and extension allow you to achieve a "quiet" upper body while you ski through bumps. A quiet upper body glides smoothly down the hill while the legs pump rapidly up and down, absorbing the bumps. When a mogul skier has a quiet upper body, he is said to have "good separation" (independence of movement between the lower body and upper body). Good separation means the legs do the absorbing work while the upper body enjoys the relatively smooth, quiet ride. It looks good. It feels good. And it allows the skier to maintain balance and control.*

Speed control

Groomed-trail skiers control speed (and direction) with turns. Bump skiers also control speed with turns. But bump skiers control speed with absorption and extension, too. Just as turns slow a skier down, so do absorption and extension slow the bump skier down. In less demanding mogul conditions (soft, rhythmic bumps on a gently-sloped trail), it's even possible for a good bump skier to control his speed primarily with absorption and extension, and hardly at all with turns. In such conditions, it's possible for the expert bumper to descend the hill without turning his skis much at all, and to still maintain control and balance through absorption and extension. Of course, this wouldn't be the way to win high turn points in competition, and competitions are always held on steeper trails that demand lots of turning as well as good absorption and extension.

A closer look at absorption and extension

As the bump skier skis over a mogul or mogul side, she bends at the ankles, knees and hips (not so much at the back) to absorb the impact. As she passes that mogul and enters the trough, she immediately extends her legs and drives her skis down into the trough. (This extension movement is her return to her tall home posture.)

*Among groomed-trail habitués, the word "separation" usually refers to upper-body counter (twisting) movements. Among mogul skiers, it refers to absorption movements. Among all skiers, it refers to the independence of upper and lower body movements.

To maintain maximum speed control and the best possible balance, the bumper uses her absorption and extension
movements to keep her skis in contact with the snow as much
as possible. When she wants to speed up, she doesn't fully
extend into every trough; she allows her skis to momentarily
leave the snow while she passes through (over) each trough.
By lessening her ski-to-snow contact, and the friction produced
by that contact, she increases her speed. The mogul skier's
adjusting of this absorption and extension is called "touch."
When a bump skier knows how to adjust her absorption and
extension for the right mix of speed and control, she is said to
have "good touch."

Extending and absorbing at a relatively fast speed, through relatively large moguls.

In a sense, absorbing and extending are just a different sort of turning. Most skiers think of turning as directing their skis left and right. But bump skiers use absorption and extension to execute a sort of "up-and-down turn." And just as left-and-right turns control speed, so do the bump skier's up-and-down turns. Another way to understand the speed-controlling aspect of absorption and extension is with our staircase analogy: just as stepping onto a stair tread controls the speed of your descent down a staircase, driving your tips down into the trough and then absorbing the impact of the bump controls the speed of your descent down a mogul field.

Aspiring bumpers just learning to absorb and extend in the moguls should **try to keep their skis on the snow as much as possible.** Every bump you ski over will throw your tips into the air. As soon as you pass the bump, however, you should immediately drive your tips down into the trough. (Again, this works hand-in-hand with your returning to home.) If you spend too much time with your skis in the air, you'll gain too much speed and you won't be able to stay in the fall line. You'll have to bail out and traverse the trail to regain control.

A narrow stance

A narrow stance will help you to absorb and extend more smoothly and effectively. With a wider stance, you're more likely to be caught in the awkward situation of your having one foot up high on a bump (absorbing) while the other foot is down low in a trough (extending). Such "altitude splits" between your two feet will throw off your coordinated and rhythmic absorption and extension movements. A narrow stance, on the other hand, will allow for simultaneous, rhythmic absorption and extension movements.

By the way, the bump skier's narrow stance also has two other advantages: one technical and one aesthetic. With your legs and feet together, you can increase the overall strength, speed and fluidity with which you turn, absorb and extend, because one leg (or foot) can actually help the other to move, and help to support the other. When you steer your feet with your boots together, for example, one foot actually helps the other foot to steer. The united whole, you see, can be greater than the sum of its separate parts.

WRONG

With a wider stance, you're more likely to be caught in the awkward situation of having one foot up high on a bump (absorbing) while the other foot is down low in a trough (extending). Such "altitude splits" between your two feet will throw off your coordinated and rhythmic absorption and extension movements.

And then there's the aesthetic reason for the narrow mogul-skiing stance: the world's mogul skiers and mogul-skiing judges all agree that it looks good. As competitive mogul skiing is a judged sport, aesthetics are relevant.

Racers and other groomed-trail experts ski with a relatively wide stance so that they'll have room between their feet and legs to create the dramatic leg and hip angles necessary for carving and "arcing" turns on groomed snow. Since mogul skiers don't do any arcing or carving in the bumps, and since the moguls themselves do a lot of the angulating for the mogul skier (remember, again, the staircase analogy), bumpers don't need space between their feet and legs. Mogul skiers are free to enjoy the advantages of a narrow stance.

Don't be confused about this narrow-stance business. Yes, a narrow stance may have its disadvantages on an alpine race course. In the moguls, however, the narrow stance is correct: it's good skiing. You may meet instructors who suggest that a wider stance is correct everywhere on the mountain. Don't listen to them. Don't take mogul-skiing advice from groomed-trail experts. Take mogul-skiing advice from mogul-skiing experts. The best mogul skiers in the world ski with their legs and feet together, and they do so for technical as well as aesthetic reasons.

Absorption and extension tips:

❊ Narrow your stance and operate your skis as if they were one unit, as if your two feet were resting on a single platform. Try keeping light but constant pressure between your two legs throughout the run:

the right knee pushing towards the left, the left knee pushing towards the right. Together, your legs will feel like a single, loaded spring, and you'll be ready for smooth, unified, fast, forceful movement.

❄ Don't wait for the mogul to flex your legs for you; initiate the absorption yourself, as you approach the bump. At higher speeds, you will need to start your absorption early, before you reach the bump. Your goal is to avoid violent impact with the mogul by smoothly and quickly absorbing that impact with your legs (not your back).

❄ Your extension is your return to your tall home posture. Remember to drive your hips up (skyward) and forward (down the hill) as you return to home. Try to maintain that shin-to-tongue contact all the way down the hill.

❄ Until you've mastered absorption and extension, try to keep your skis in contact with the snow as much as possible. As you pass the bump, immediately drive your tips down into the trough.
This will help to maximize your balance and minimize your speed.

❄ Don't underestimate your skis' ability to fit into narrow, deep troughs, and to function well there. In big, tight moguls, you will need to quickly and aggressively absorb and extend. When faced with narrow, deep troughs, you should have faith in your extension technique: just stuff those ski tips down into each of those troughs. You'll be amazed at how extending will smooth out your skiing and make those tough-looking troughs manageable.

❄ At high speeds, absorption and extension will mean a rapid, piston-like, up-and-down pumping of the legs. At low speeds, gravity will help to push your skis back down onto the snow after you pass each bump. At higher speeds, gravity won't help; you'll need to push your skis down onto the snow, into the troughs, with aggressive quickness and force.

You can practice absorption and extension while traversing a mogul field.

The Drill

There are two good ways to practice absorption and extension. The first is to do it while slowly traversing a mogul field.
While traversing, you'll be able to practice absorption and
extension without worrying about controlling your speed or
making turns: worries you would have were you skiing straight
down the fall line. As you become increasingly comfortable
with absorption and extension in a traverse, you can gradually speed up your traverse by pointing your skis farther and
farther downhill. Eventually, you'll be absorbing and extending
right down the fall line.

The second good way to practice absorption and extension
is to do it down the fall line on just a few gentle moguls that

lead onto groomed, gentle terrain. Knowing that you'll soon be able to safely stop yourself on gentle, groomed terrain, you won't need to worry about gaining too much speed while you descend the bumpy fall line.

A new means of control

As you practice absorption and extension, you'll discover a new means of maintaining your balance and controlling your speed. Gradually, you'll bring this new means of control into your skiing on increasingly difficult mogul runs. As with everything, start small, then work your way up to the more difficult mogul trails. As you gain mastery, you'll be amazed at how absorption and extension will allow you to ski smoothly and in control through big bumps and deep troughs.

5. CHOOSING YOUR LINE

In mogul competition, you must demonstrate, among other things, your ability to ski a straight line. When you ski a straight line in the moguls, your feet move laterally (left and right) beneath your torso, while your torso travels straight down the hill. You don't meander about the mogul field. You don't allow the terrain to dictate your path. Regardless of what the mountain throws at you, you move your torso straight down the hill, while your legs absorb and extend through the dramatic ups and downs and maintain a regular turning rhythm.

Aspiring recreational bumpers should also ski a straight line through the bumps. Your moving your torso straight down the mogul trail's fall line while your skis turn beneath you is called "skiing the zipper line," and zipper-line skiing is the very definition of mogul skiing. The ability to ski the fall line in the bumps separates the mogul skiers from those who know only groomed-trail and mogul-survival skills.

Were I to spin, Royal-Christie, pole-flip and hand-spring my way down a groomed trail on a pair of old ballet skis, most groomed-trail aficionados would not call this skiing of mine "alpine skiing." They might call it "ballet skiing" or "freestyle skiing" or "hot-dogging," but not "alpine skiing." Similarly, when a skier meanders back and forth across the fall line on a mogul field, mogul skiers do not consider this mogul skiing. To put it all another way: among mogul skiers, there is no need for the term "fall-line mogul skiing," because fall-line mogul skiing is the only sort of mogul skiing there is. Real mogul skiing doesn't exist outside of the fall line. You see, just as alpine racing has influenced and defined recreational alpine skiing, competitive mogul skiing has influenced and defined recreational mogul skiing.

There is still the question, however, of exactly where you should direct your skis while you move your torso straight down the hill. The answer depends upon, among other things, the sort of bumps you're skiing.

Choosing your line through uniform bumps

When a trail with good snow is skied by good bump skiers making rapid, rhythmic turns, uniform bumps develop.
Machine-made bumps (bumps made by a grooming machine)
are also very uniform. Uniform bumps are similar to one
another in size and shape. They're relatively rounded, and
they're arranged closely together in a regular, orderly, check-
erboard pattern.

*Uniform bumps pretty much tell you
where and when to turn your skis; they
choose your line for you.*

When you ski uniform bumps, whether those bumps were made by good bump skiers or by a machine, choosing your line (path) is easy, very intuitive. Uniform bumps pretty much tell you where and when to turn your skis; they choose your line for you. You simply send your body straight down the fall line and turn your skis where the troughs tell you to turn. If you can turn where the troughs tell you to turn, and keep your skis on the snow (through absorption and extension) during most of your descent, you'll ski these uniform bumps well.

Perfectly uniform bumps, however, are hard to find, especially in the east, where the snow is not so soft and deep. Even good mogul fields have at least small sections of irregular bumps, and navigating irregular bumps requires special line-choice techniques.

Choosing your line through irregular bumps

When a trail is skied by less skilled skiers who make irregular, arrhythmic turns, irregular moguls will develop. (Inferior technique, you see, produces inferior moguls as well as inferior mogul skiers.) Irregular bumps can also form when a bump trail is left un-groomed for too long a period of time. Irregular bumps have some or all of the following characteristics:

❄ *Widely varying shapes and sizes;*
❄ *Sharp angles;*
❄ *Widely varying distances from one another (they sit in no particular, regular relationship to one another; they have no rhythm);*
❄ *Long, slick, flat patches between them;*
❄ *Troughs that turn too abruptly;*
❄ *Overly long troughs that turn too gradually.*

Skiing irregular bumps can be punishing. When it's done incorrectly, it often involves sudden deceleration and jarring impact with abrupt bumps, and sudden acceleration between widely-spaced bumps. With the right choice of line, however, you can ski irregular bumps smoothly and without punishing yourself.

In irregular bumps, you should always look for the smooth line that won't be punishing to ski. There's an old Taoist story about a gifted butcher who never had to sharpen the blade of his cleaver. Lesser butchers hacked and strong-armed their way through the hard bones of the animal carcasses, and these butchers' blades were always in need of sharpening. But the gifted Taoist butcher

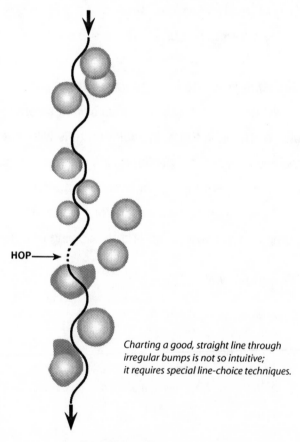

HOP

Charting a good, straight line through irregular bumps is not so intuitive; it requires special line-choice techniques.

knew how to maneuver his blade through the soft, forgiving places in the carcass. He never struck bone and never dulled his blade.

When you ski irregular bumps, you should be like this Taoist master. Don't just ski through the same old troughs, in the path of all the butchers who came before you. Find the soft, forgiving line that other skiers haven't yet discovered. Ski the least punishing line, the line that won't dull your blade.

A line of your own

Most skiers try to ski irregular bumps as they would ski uniform bumps. That is, most skiers, regardless of whether they're skiing uniform or irregular bumps, turn only where the troughs tell them to turn. In irregular bumps, therefore, these skiers ski irregularly! They pick up too much speed in overly long troughs, and they slam into every abrupt bump.

But skilled mogul skiers know that irregular bumps must be skied differently. Skilled bump skiers know to not take turning directions from irregular moguls, to not slavishly ski the punishing troughs formed by other skiers. Skilled mogul skiers find their own smooth line through irregular bumps. And one way they do this is by skiing up high on the bump, rather than down low in the trough. Because they know how to ski high on the bump, good mogul skiers are free from the tyranny of irregular, punishing trough lines.

Don't get me wrong; most irregular mogul fields do have sections of uniform bumps here and there. So, even in irregular bumps, you'll make many of your turns in the trough line. But you should always be ready and able to leave the troughs when you spot trouble, and re-enter the troughs where they become rhythmic and smooth again. Good skiing through irregular bumps requires an artful combination of skiing in the troughs and skiing high on the moguls. And there really is an art to it, an aspect that will come from you rather than from any how-to book or instructor. I can, however, give you a couple of tools to use in pursuit of your art.

Trough hopping

In chapter four, I described how an expert bump skier will allow his skis to leave the snow between bumps (as he passes through the trough) in order to increase his speed. Expert bumpers allow their skis to leave the snow for other reasons, too. They allow their skis to leave the snow in order to avoid lousy snow conditions: in order to skip over sharp-turning troughs, for example.

During an average bump run, you'll make most of your turns in the troughs. During this same average bump run, however, you'll encounter problem troughs: icy troughs that turn too sharply and end with an abrupt bump; or long, straight troughs without enough turn in them to allow you to control your speed. Because troughs like these are punishing and dangerous to ski, you shouldn't ski them.

A Trough Hop

HOP   LAND

One way to avoid a problem trough is to hop over it. Trough hopping is one of the techniques that can turn an average bump skier into a great bump skier. When you learn to hop over a problem trough and land up high on the bump, you elevate your bump skiing to a new level of expertise. Suddenly, you're free from the trough line, free to ski where most others don't even think of skiing.

The drill

Find, in the fall line, two small moguls that lead onto groomed, intermediate terrain. These two bumps should be six to eight feet apart. Ski over the first bump with just moderate speed. Be sure to maintain your balance. Don't let your weight fall back over the tails of your skis, and don't completely absorb the bump. As you crest the bump, use your leg muscles to pop off of the top of the bump, clear

You can first learn and practice the trough hop while traversing, or partially traversing, a gentle mogul field.

the trough, and land on the uphill face of the second bump. Be sure to land on the uphill face of the second bump, near the bump's top, not on the very top, and not on the downhill (back) side of the bump. Your landing on the uphill face of the second bump will control the speed you pick up in the air over the trough. If you land too low, near the trough, you're likely to be tripped up and dumped by the bump itself. And if you land on the very top or downhill side of the bump, you'll gain speed rather than control it.

After you become comfortable with this maneuver, try turning your skis while you're in the air, over the trough, so that you land in the midst of a turn, on your edges. This edge set, high on the bump, will control your speed even further. Practice this trough hopping on your two practice bumps until you're comfortable with it. When you become proficient at trough hopping, it won't feel or look as abrupt as the word "hopping" suggests. It will look like smooth mogul skiing. Your skis will simply leave the snow between bumps as you glide from one high spot to the next.

Incorporate your new trough hopping ability into your bump skiing. Be sure to ease your way into this on a trail that's not too steep, and on bumps that aren't too big. Take note of how well you can control your speed by landing on edge on the uphill face of a bump. Big, soft bumps make an especially forgiving landing that will help to control speed especially well. Use your new trough-hopping ability to hop over problem troughs, and to negotiate misplaced bumps that sit squarely in your line.

Flat spots and rhythm maintenance

Irregular mogul fields often have flat spots that tell you, if you're taking turning directions from the terrain, to stop turning for a while and to either point your skis straight down the trail or to skid them sideways for a long distance. Of course, you don't want to do either.

These flat spots are made by skiers who don't maintain a regular turning rhythm, skiers who get spooked by the steeps and then side-skid for long distances down the trail. You don't want to take direction from these skiers. But that's what you're doing when you obey a flat spot that tells you to stop turning.

Here's an important bump skiing rule – a mantra, even – that I've been suggesting but haven't yet explicitly stated: **don't let irregular bumps dictate your turning rhythm.** Maintain your turning rhythm, or speed it up, even when the trail isn't telling you to turn. Even on flat ice, your cranking a few quick turns will help to control your speed. And it'll look good to the judges and keep your turn points high, if you happen to be competing. And, remember: flat spots are usually icy, so it's especially important for you to not overweight your ski tails. On ice, your tails will quickly slip out from under you if you overweight them even just slightly.

Instead of skidding down flat spots and slamming into abrupt bumps...

...try hopping and landing.

RIGHT

You'll often find an abrupt trough and a big, soft bump sitting at the bottom of a flat spot. This is because the side-skidding skiers who formed the flat spot scraped a lot of snow down the hill and that snow gathered just below the flat spot. If you try to ski through this abrupt trough at speed and with your skis on the snow, the trough may prove too abrupt to be skied smoothly. A very abrupt trough can turn your skis completely sideways (perpendicular to the fall line), stop them short, and throw you over the handlebars for a face-plant.

You should use your trough-hopping technique not only to avoid problem troughs that lie between bumps, but also to avoid these abrupt troughs that typically lie between flat spots and bumps. In this case, you won't be hopping from one bump to the next, but from a flat spot to a bump. This technique will allow you to avoid the abrupt trough and to use the soft bump to control the speed you pick up on the flat spot and in the air.

Look for subtleties, trust your hunches

As I've already said, line choice is an art. Feel free to venture beyond the limited definitions and techniques I've described in this chapter. And you should always pay attention to subtleties and trust your hunches.

Seemingly small things – minor temperature changes, a dusting of new snow, a little skier traffic – can significantly change the character of a mogul run for better or worse. The mogul run you ski during any given afternoon will almost certainly ski differently the next morning, for example, even when the trail hasn't been groomed or otherwise touched. Sometimes, just your own repeated skiing down a particular line can be enough to change the way that line skis, and change the way you want to ski that line. A particular trough may become too rutted and abrupt after several runs, for example, and you may want to start hopping that trough and skiing high on the bump in future runs.

The advice I've given you in this chapter is basic advice meant only to get you started. Ultimately, every mogul field is unique, and every individual mogul is unique and in a state of perpetual change. As you practice the art of line choice, pay attention to subtleties, trust your hunches, and be ready to respond with your own new ways of doing things.

A Line-Choice Sequence

Here, a wide, awkwardly shaped bump sits between me and a nice, uniform trough line. To avoid an abrupt, sideways slam into the bump, I hop onto it (photos 1 and 2).

In order to control my speed and sync up my turns with the uniform trough line I'm about to enter, I sneak in a quick turn on the back of the bump (photo 3).

Then I'm able to drop into the rhythmic trough line (photo 4) and continue down the obvious path.

6.   EYES ON THE BIG PICTURE

If, while you ski the moguls, you look at only the mogul immediately before you, your balance will suffer, your nerves will suffer, and your choice of lines will suffer. In the bumps, the average expert skier tends to get too caught-up with the small picture, tends to limit his vision too much. Bump skiers, while they ski even the trickiest bumps, don't stare at, or worry too much about, the bump beneath their skis or even the bump immediately in front of them. Instead, they look three to five bumps down the hill. They keep their eyes on the big picture.

Even in the trickiest bumps, skilled bump skiers look three to five bumps down the hill.

The Drill

On a groomed, intermediate trail, look downhill along the fall line you'll be skiing, and select a landmark in that line. The landmark might be anywhere from 50 to 100 yards away. It might be a fencepost, a distinctive looking tree, a chairlift stanchion, or any other stationary object.

Ski slowly toward your landmark, and keep your eyes on it throughout your descent. At first, you may not be able to keep your eyes on the landmark throughout the run; you may be too tempted to look down at the snow a few yards in front of your skis. With repetition of the exercise, however, you'll learn to trust your skis' ability to absorb minor irregularities in the snow, and you'll learn to trust your lower, peripheral vision.

Once you've become comfortable with this exercise, try the following. From the top of a gentle mogul trail, study the first three bumps in your line, then fix your eyes on the third bump. Now ski the trail and, throughout the run, keep your eyes fixed three bumps ahead of the bump beneath your skis. If you're comfortable with looking three bumps ahead, try four. If you're comfortable with four, try five.

How and why it works

Just as you can worry too much about a scratch on your new car, an off-handed comment made by your boss, or how you look in a pair of jeans, you can worry too much about the particular shape of the mogul over which you're skiing.

Because your skis, when used properly, can absorb a lot of snow irregularity (skis can smoothly absorb far more snow irregularity and impact than most skiers realize), you don't need to stare at and worry about the unique particulars of the bump you're about to ski over. This is one of the secrets of relaxing and skiing quickly and smoothly through the bumps.

Don't worry about the exact shape of the bump or trough beneath your skis. If you worry too much about the bump beneath your skis, you'll have too limited a perspective; you won't see the whole picture. So don't even bother to look at that one bump or trough beneath your skis. Relax. Give your nerves a rest. If you're looking four bumps down the hill while you ski, you saw, four bumps ago, that bump or trough over which you're now skiing. And you saw enough of it then to know how to ski it. Trust your memory; you'll remember what you saw four bumps ago. And trust your equipment; your skis will absorb minor irregularities in the snow.

Keeping your eyes on the big picture will not only help you feel more relaxed in the bumps, but will also improve your balance. Your balance depends on the visual information you receive through your eyes. If you limit this visual information by looking down toward your ski tips, away from the horizon, your balance will also be limited. If, however, you take in more visual information by directing your eyesight out beyond your ski tips, up toward the horizon, you'll improve your balance. The more you can see of the landscape ahead of you, the more able you are to maintain good balance.

If, while you ski the moguls, you look at only the mogul immediately before you, your balance will suffer, your nerves will suffer, and your choice of lines will suffer.

Keeping your eyes on the big picture will also promote a good upper-body position: it will help you maintain an upright torso. When you drop your eyesight down toward the ground immediately in front of you, you're more likely to drop your head forward, too, and to bend at the back. Of course, if you do this, you lose your tall, home mogul-skiing posture. If you direct your vision farther down the slope, however, you'll tend to hold your head more upright (less bend in the neck), and it'll be easier for you to hold your torso upright, too.

Finally, keeping your eyes on the big picture will also help you to choose your line through the bumps. You can't plan your next three turns through the bumps if you don't know what the next three bumps look like. Looking farther down the hill gives you a chance to plan your turns (choose your line) ahead of time.

7. POLING AND HAND POSITION

The bumps are always conspiring to throw you into the back seat. For this reason, the bump skier pays special attention to every possible means of keeping his weight centered over his skis. These means include poling and hand position.

The mogul skier's definition of good poling and hand position is pretty much the same as the groomed-trail skier's definition. The mogul skier's definition of good poling and hand position, however, is more emphatic. Aspiring bumpers often find that they have to tune up their poling skills (get better at what they already do) for the moguls, because the moguls leave less room for poling and hand-position error. Good poling and hand position help you to maintain balance, and balance is tougher to maintain in the bumps than it is on the flats. Sloppy poling that might not have prevented you from being an expert on groomed trails could still prove a handicap in the bumps. To put it another way: poling and hand position are more exact and demanding a science for the mogul skier than they are for the average groomed-trail expert.

Poling in the bumps

A time-honored hand-positioning rule holds true for bump skiers: if you pretend that you're holding before you a tray of drinks, your hands will be in a good position for bump skiing.

They'll be about shoulder width apart. And they'll be in your lower peripheral vision as you look down the trail. Try to avoid swinging your hand far out to your side or back when you pole. With your hand out to your side or back, your weight is

By keeping your hands in front of you and reaching down the hill, you'll maintain better balance in the bumps.

more easily thrown back. In general, you should reach down the hill with your hands, in the direction in which you're traveling. By keeping your hands in front of you, you'll better resist the temptations to crouch and lean back, and you'll be better able to drive your hips up (skyward) and forward (down the hill) as you extend into each trough.

Ideally, your poling movement involves little more than a subtle flick of the wrist, while your hands and arms remain pretty much stationary. This is all part of the bump skier's effort to maintain a quiet, balanced upper body while his legs pump rapidly through the moguls like a piston.

Pole plants, you should know, are not meant to support a lot of weight. In other words: you should avoid leaning very heavily on your planted pole while you ski. Your leaning heavily on your pole while you ski can increase your chances of injury, and it's not good skiing. This is true for all downhill skiing. The pole shouldn't be used as a physical crutch during the descent.

When you plant your ski pole, you should just tap the snow with the tip of your pole. This tap provides you with a third point of snow contact. (Your two skis are the first and second points of contact.) Without your consciously thinking about it, this extra point of snow contact helps you to survey and understand the wildly undulating terrain over which you're skiing. The pole plant provides your brain with information that helps you maintain your balance.

Finally, regular, rhythmic pole plants are also vital to regular, rhythmic turns. In irregular moguls, which tempt you to turn with an irregular rhythm, regular pole plants will help you to maintain your rhythmic turning, which is vital to your maintaining control in the bumps.

Mogul-poling miscellany:

✱ *Because pole plants initiate turns, and because the bump skier most often starts his turn somewhere on the bump, you will most often plant your pole on the top or back of the bump.*

✱ *Many bump skiers use short ski poles, and you may want to as well.*
For more information about this equipment choice, see chapter 10.

8. AIR

Jumping and performing aerial maneuvers in the moguls is more difficult than jumping in a terrain park or on some other groomed trail. In a terrain park, you have the luxury of approaching your jump on smooth, groomed snow, so you have plenty of opportunity to adjust and secure your balance before takeoff. There are no bumps to throw you off balance at the last moment. The terrain park also offers a smooth, mogul-free landing.

In the bumps, however, you have very little time for setting up before you jump, and very little time for recovering after you land. One second you're making fast turns, and rapidly absorbing and extending. The next second, you're in the air performing your maneuver. And the next, you're landing among more bumps and you must immediately resume your rapid turning, absorbing and extending. In the bumps, you also need to land on exactly the right spot on your landing bump, in order to control your speed.

Over the last ten or so years, the organizers of mogul competitions have eliminated some of these jumping difficulties with shovel-built jumps and smoothed landing areas. Even with these well-designed jumps, however, mogul-specific jumping techniques remain useful and important. And, of course, these techniques will always remain useful and important for recreational mogul skiers who jump in skier-made mogul fields, and not from shovel-made jumps.

Basics first

Before you attempt to jump in the moguls, learn jumping basics in a terrain park or on some other groomed trail. Start by taking small jumps at low speeds. Good balance is vital. When you leave the snow, your weight should be centered over your skis: not too far back, not too far forward, and not leaning to either side. A slight imbalance on takeoff will be magnified in the air. If you find yourself off balance before takeoff, don't jump. If you can, absorb the lip (top) of the jump and keep your skis on the ground. Trying to jump while you're off balance will only throw you further off balance, which could result in your landing in any imaginable position. There's a considerable possibility for injury here, so be careful.

Before you attempt to jump in the moguls, learn jumping basics in a terrain park or on some other groomed trail.

As you ski up the face of your jump, don't allow the jump to push you into the back seat. As you crest the lip of the jump, use your leg muscles to push yourself skyward, straight up. As you push yourself skyward (as you "pop" off of the lip), keep your hands in front of you to prevent yourself from leaning back. If you find yourself habitually leaning back on takeoff, try gently thrusting your fists forward in the air as you pop. This will help to keep you from leaning back. But it can also throw your weight too far forward, so be careful to not overcompensate.

Although steeper slopes may look more intimidating, a steep landing is a safe landing, because it absorbs more impact. These days, many ski areas have terrain parks built by grooming machine operators who don't understand the importance of a steep landing hill. Many of these operators build jumps that have the potential to throw skiers and riders remarkably high into the air, but have either an inadequate, gently sloped landing, or an adequately steep landing that is too short and therefore too easily overshot.

Landing on a gentle slope can be dangerous and painful. It can strain, among other things, the arches of your feet, your knees and your back. Don't trust the grooming-machine operator who built your local terrain park. (Many of these operators don't even ski or ride.) Before jumping, examine your jumps carefully and make sure that the landing areas are sufficiently steep to absorb your landing impact. Make sure that you'll be able to reach your landing area without overshooting it. And make sure, before you jump, that you can see the landing slope, or that you have a friend who can see it and signal you when it's clear. You don't want to crash into other skiers or riders.

Traffic is another problem with terrain parks. Parks are often filled with skiers and riders jumping one immediately after the other, with little regard for what might happen if the guy in front crashes. Regardless of how others ski or ride in the park, you should wait as long as it takes to get a clear run at your jump.

Once you're comfortable with jumping and landing, start with the most basic maneuvers. The spread eagle is a good place to start. You might try dry-land practice before you try the maneuvers on snow. Trampolines and low walls are good for this. Trampolines can, however, be as dangerous as ski jumps. Also, remember that jumping on snow while you're wearing skis and boots will feel different from bouncing on a trampoline or leaping off a low wall in your sneakers or bare feet. Your body will move more slowly when it's burdened with heavy ski equipment.

Throwing air in the bumps

Once you've practiced your jumping in a terrain park or on some other groomed slope, and you feel ready to try jumping in the bumps, you'll need to plan carefully. You'll need to find a bump that will kick you up high enough for you to perform your trick. But you don't want an air bump that's too abruptly steep, as an overly steep bump will throw you off balance.

You'll also need a second bump on which to land. A good landing bump has a soft uphill face that will absorb your impact and help you to control your speed. Take the time to find the right two bumps before trying your jump.

As you pop off the lip of your air bump, don't lean back over the tails of your skis, and don't lean too far forward. If you're off balance as you're leaving the air bump, abort the mission; absorb your air bump as much as you can (don't pop from the lip), and try to just stay close to the ground and regain your balance.

Remember to control your speed before takeoff. Take off with no more speed than you need to complete your maneuver and reach your landing bump. On a steep mogul trail with a big jump or air bump, you'll often not need too much speed at all to get the job done.

Be sure to land on the uphill face of your landing bump with your skis turned to one side. This way, you'll be on edge when you land, which will further control your speed. Always land on the uphill face of your landing bump. Landing in a trough or on the very top or downhill side of a bump will more often than not result in a loss of speed-control and balance. Of course, if you're landing on a prepared landing area (like the landing areas you're likely to encounter in competition), you'll enjoy landing in smoothed, softened snow.

And here's another piece of advice about jumping in the moguls: **you don't have to do it!** If you like mogul skiing, but have no desire to jump, just do what you want to do: ski bumps and don't bother with air. I know plenty of fantastic rec-reational bump skiers who simply don't bother with air.

A few words about a few classic aerial maneuvers

These days, the best mogul skiers are performing all sorts of difficult, inverted aerial maneuvers. These advanced tricks are beyond the scope of this book. The brief notes below are meant to simply get you started with the easier, safer tricks that mogul skiers have been performing for years.

By the way, if you happen to be a terrain park habitué who's comfortable in the air and knows all sorts of spectacular aerial maneuvers, you've come to mogul skiing with an advan-tage over other good skiers who are new to jumping. It won't take much for you to adjust your jumping to the moguls. But back to those classic tricks.

Spread eagle

✺   *A relatively easy maneuver.*

✺   *Keep your legs straight.*

✺   *Be sure your groin muscles are limber, to avoid muscle pulls.*

Twister

✳   *A relatively easy maneuver, although it does involve a
     twisting (legs) and counter-twisting (torso) motion for which you
     must develop the knack.*

✳   *As you twist your skis in one direction, twist your shoulders in the
     opposite direction. Then, as you bring your skis back to center, bring
     your shoulders back to center.*

✳   *A good maneuver to master on dry land first.*

✳   *Multiple twisters (double, triple, quad) are classic mogul maneuvers.*

Tip-dropping maneuvers

❈   *Moderately difficult.*

❈   *With tip-dropping maneuvers, you'll need enough altitude to drop one or both tips toward the snow without catching a tip and sending yourself for a violent face-plant.*

Daffy

Iron Cross

Helicopter / 360

❋   *A relatively difficult maneuver.*

❋   *Difficult to land in tight bumps, because you lose sight of your landing area as you spin.*

❋   *Your head and shoulders should lead the rest of your body through the spin. Avoid the temptation to stop rotating your head and shoulders partway through the spin. Just keep looking around the corner until you complete your rotation.*

❋   *As with all of these tricks, be sure to completely master it on a groomed trail before attempting it in the moguls.*

Learning inverted maneuvers

Mogul skiers interested in learning inverted aerial maneuvers should do so at a freestyle training facility. Freestyle facilities have trampoline-and-harness setups, water ramps and other special equipment, as well as good coaches, all of which will make your learning as safe as it can be. While there aren't a huge number of freestyle training facilities in the world, they do exist. Some ski academies offer dry-land, freestyle training, as do some summer ski camps.

9.   COMPETITIVE MOGUL SKIING

In competition, the alpine racer has only one ultimate goal: to ski through the race course faster than everyone else. Speed is all that matters in racing. In competitive mogul skiing, however, speed accounts for only 25% of a competitor's overall score. The quality of the bump skier's line and turns accounts for 50%. And two aerial maneuvers account for the remaining 25%. Like alpine racers, mogul competitors are clocked for run time. Line, turn and air points are determined by judges.

The courses

Most mogul courses are two to three times the length of a football field (200 to 300 yards long), and 10 to 15 yards wide. Dual-format courses are comprised of two side-by-side courses of about 10 yards in width.

A mogul course has either skier-made or machine-made bumps on it, and two jumping areas. The mogul competitor is typically required to perform two jumps per run, but a single jumping area may have two or three jumps sitting side-by-side, so that the skier may choose the one she wishes to hit.

In the '80s, when I competed in mogul events run by the USSA (then the United States Ski Association, now the United States Ski and Snowboard Association), mogul courses had only skier-made bumps. There were no machine-made bumps, and competitors performed their two aerial maneuvers by jumping off of two moguls. These days, the bumps on courses are often perfectly patterned and shaped, machine-made bumps. The jumps are made with grooming machines and shovels. And the landing areas are at least partially flattened and padded with soft snow.

It could be argued that machine-made bumps have removed some of the artfulness and variety from competitive mogul skiing. But it's not true that the custom-made jumps and groomed landing areas have made the aerial component any easier; they've simply upped the ante. In the eighties, even upright, quad maneuvers (a triple-twister-spread, for example) were unusual, because skier-made moguls didn't provide the air time needed for quad tricks. Helicopters (360s) were also relatively uncommon in mogul competition back then, because they were so difficult to land on the old courses.

Today, however, quad maneuvers, 360s, iron-cross-360s, iron-cross back flips, and twisting flips are performed regularly in World Cup mogul competition. So jumping in competitive mogul skiing hasn't become easier; it has become more aerial and spectacular.

Format

There are two formats for mogul skiing competition: single and dual. In the single format, competitors ski the course

(Illustration A) one at a time. In the dual / elimination format (Illustration B), skiers ski side-by-side, two at a time, competing only against one another. For some contests, a skier must first qualify with a single-format run, and then compete head-to-head in dual-format runs.

With a purely single-format competition, one great run can

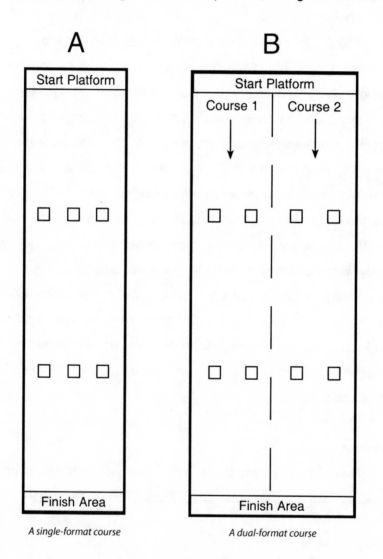

A single-format course   A dual-format course

be enough to win an event. But this is never so with the dual format. With duals, a skier must have multiple, consecutive, head-to-head victories in order to repeatedly eliminate other competitors and win the event.

Line, turns and air

Judges reward the bump competitor for skiing a straight line; they don't like to see a skier picking her way around the course, meandering left and right. When the mogul competitor skis a straight line, her torso moves straight down the course while her skis turn rapidly beneath her. Mogul competitors are also rewarded for the quality of their turns. Judges award the highest scores to those skiers who make the greatest number of fast, smooth, fluid turns.

As I mentioned above, the mogul competitor is required to perform two jumping maneuvers (airs) with each run. The competitor's air score is a product of the difficulty of the maneuvers he performs and the proficiency and style with which he performs them.

Climbing the competitive ranks

In the United States, young bump skiers compete throughout the ski season at regional ski meets sanctioned by the USSA. These meets are held at ski areas all over the country in a number of different geographical regions. Each season, the USSA invites the best skiers from each region to compete in national-level events.

Through this system, the USSA identifies the best bump skiers in the country, and invites them to represent the United States at international-level contests: Nor Am and World Cup competitions run by FIS (International Ski Federation). Every four years, the USSA invites the best bumpers on the U.S. Ski Team (our World Cup competitors) to represent the United States at the Olympics. Olympian bumpers are the absolute best of the best. Since mogul skiing became an Olympic sport in the early 1990s, these great American skiers have included Olympic medalists Nelson Carmichael, Donna Weinbrecht, Jonny Moseley, Shannon Bahrke and Travis Mayer.

You can get more information about regional and national USSA-sanctioned mogul competition by contacting the USSA at:

> U.S. Ski and Snowboard Association
> Box 100
> 1500 Kearns Blvd.
> Park City, UT 84060

You can also find the USSA on the Web at www.ussa.org. Canadian bumpers can get competition information from the Canadian Freestyle Ski Association (www.freestyleski.com).

Local, open mogul competitions

Plenty of ski areas, large and small, hold their own, open mogul competitions that any skier of any age can enter without a lot of fanfare. Usually, you're required only to fill out a registration form on the morning of the event and to pay a nominal registration fee.

These relatively casual competitions are often held annually in the spring, and they can be a lot of fun. Each ski season, I travel around northern New England and compete in several of these little contests. Most of them are structured to recognize winners across multiple age categories, with separate male and female categories. And the prizes are sometimes really good. It's not uncommon for winners to receive new skis, for example. Other common prizes include trophies, ski clothing, goggles, ski bags and gift certificates.

In the northeast, where I live, two of the biggest of these contests are held in the spring at Killington (Vermont) and Sunday River (Maine). Both of these contests are two-day events, and both draw a lot of spectators and skilled competitors. Attitash (New Hampshire), Sugarbush (Vermont), Jay Peak (Vermont), Stowe (Vermont) and a number of other areas in the northeast have been known to hold fun, open, one-day contests in the spring. If you're interested in competing in an open event, check the ski area's on-line events calendar for scheduling and registration details.

When you register for the event, ask about special house rules that the local judges may be observing. As these contests are casual events, the judging can be quirky. For example, while USSA rules require two different aerial maneuvers within each run, some local events allow you to perform the same maneuver twice. In this case, you'll score the highest if you perform your most difficult maneuver twice, because you won't be penalized for repeating the trick.

And, then, some local events require only one jump per run. Some give each skier only one run through the course. Some give two runs. Some give three. And sometimes it all depends on the weather that happens to be moving in on that spring afternoon. As I said, many of these open mogul contests are pretty casual events.

10. MOGUL-SKIING EQUIPMENT

I've already suggested that the mogul skier's equipment needs are as unique as her skiing techniques. Here are a few equipment tips for the aspiring mogul skier.

Skis

If you're committed to improving your mogul skiing, consider buying yourself a pair of mogul skis. Dramatically shaped skis are not ideal for bump skiing. Yes, it's true that most skiers use shaped skis these days, and that most expert skiers take their shaped skis into the bumps at least every now and then. And it's also true that some shaped skis are okay in the moguls. Mogul skis, however, will allow you to turn more easily and smoothly in the bumps. They'll give you an appropriate combination of turn-quickness and stability. They'll smooth out your absorption and extension. And they'll be less likely to interfere with one another (particularly at the tips) when you ski with a narrow mogul skier's stance.

Mogul skis are relatively straight (less shaped), which is appropriate for rotary-powered turns. Many of today's new bump skis also have "twin tips" (the tails are slightly turned up). Twin tips help the ski turn quickly, because a turned up tail is less likely to hook-up in the snow. The turned up tail releases more easily when you apply rotary force to the ski.

Most bump skis with twin tips have only slightly turned-up tails that are made for fast, rotary-powered turns, while terrain-park skis have dramatically turned up tails that are made for skiing backwards. Mogul skis are also designed for smooth mogul absorption, and for withstanding the stresses of mogul impact.

Over the last two or three years, mogul skis have been made with a bit more shape to them, a bit more of a side cut, than in years past. These more shaped mogul skis are the most versatile mogul skis ever made; that is, with these more shaped models, you can enjoy maximum performance in the bumps as well as a bit of carving on groomed trails. If you can't afford multiple pairs of skis, or don't enjoy running to the car or ski locker to switch skis between runs, and you want to enjoy both bump skiing and all-mountain skiing, a pair of these more shaped, more versatile mogul skis might be just what you're looking for.

Most ski manufacturers make bump skis, but you should start your shopping early. Mogul skis are generally produced in limited numbers. They can be difficult to find in shops, and manufacturers tend to quickly run out of stock. Do some research on line, and call around to your local shops to explore your mogul ski options.

You may also be able to find discounted mogul skis for sale, or up for auction, on the Internet. Many of the mogul skis I've seen on-line are one or two seasons old, but unused and still in the plastic wrappers. And many of these skis are selling for less than half the original retail price.

Boots

A good bump-skiing boot is just a little less stiff than most top-of-the-line racing boots. Most top-of-the-line racing boots allow too little ankle flexibility for bump skiing, and they're punishing on the bump skier's shins.

The boot that is second-most-stiff in most boot manufacturers' line-ups is usually still considered a high-performance racing boot or a high-performance all-mountain boot. These "second-tier racing boots" usually offer a balance of ankle flexibility and performance that is just right for the bumps. And the extra padding in these boots often makes them warmer and more comfortable than top-of-the-line racing boots.

I don't recommend boots that are more flexible or soft than second-tier racing boots. Skiing too soft a boot in the moguls is like driving a car with a cushy, soft suspension – say, a big, old Cadillac – through a tight autocross course: you just won't get the responsiveness you need.

Of course, this boot advice still leaves many boot brands for you to choose from. Choose the boot that fits you well, the boot you find most comfortable. And try to get a snug, high-performance fit. You won't get high performance from your high-performance boots if your fit is too loose and your feet slide around inside.

Orthotics

Orthotics (custom insoles) enhance the connection between your feet and your skis by removing the wiggle room in your boots. With orthotics, you're more tightly connected to your skis, so your skis respond more quickly and precisely to your commands.

Orthotics keep your feet warmer by improving your blood circulation. And they protect you from straining your arches on abrupt landings. For these reasons, I highly recommend orthotics for mogul skiers and all downhill skiers. If you own orthotics, be sure to bring them with you when you go shopping for boots. To get the best boot fit, you'll want to try on the boots with the orthotics in place.

Poles

Like many mogul skiers, I ski with short poles. The reason for short poles is simple. In the bumps, you'll often plant your pole during full absorption. Because you plant your pole when your body is relatively close to the snow, a long pole can force your hand too high into the air, and this can disrupt your otherwise smooth, fast poling and throw off your balance. With a short pole, you don't have to reach too high into the air. You can better maintain your hand position and your balance.

A good pole length for the moguls is about one grip's length shorter than you'd typically use for groom-trail skiing.

The groomed-trail rule of thumb for pole length is to ski with a pole that produces a right angle between your vertical upper arm and your forearm, when you stand up tall and plant that pole in the snow. My poles are a full seven inches shorter than those recommended for me by this rule of thumb. Many bump skiers share my preference for short poles, but some do not. You should experiment with different pole lengths and choose the length you like best. Just know that the groomed-trail rule of thumb for pole length does not apply to bump skiers.

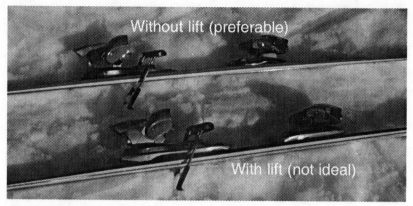

Bindings without lifts (top) are best for mogul skiing.

Equipment miscellany

No binding spacers / lifts – Many mogul skiers use bindings that are mounted directly to the skis, with no lifts in between. Lifts are meant to prevent "booting out" (hitting the side of your boot on the snow) during hard carving. Since mogul skiers don't do any carving (not while they're in the bumps, anyway) they don't need lifts. Without lifts, the bump skier benefits from a slightly lower center of gravity, which helps him to maintain better balance.

Ski pants – Be sure to choose ski pants that allow for bump skiing's dramatic ranges of motion. (Think of full absorption, and the spread eagle and daffy aerial maneuvers.) Mogul competitors and many recreational mogul skiers prefer pants that have distinctive markings on the knees or upper shins; these markings visually accentuate, for judges and spectators, the bump skier's rapid leg motion.

Supportive underwear – Male bump skiers should wear either a jock or supportive undershorts. Female bump skiers may want to wear a sports bra. The impact of big bumps and abrupt landings can deliver painful jerks to unsupported body parts. You won't always eliminate all of that impact with perfect absorption and extension.

Dress for a workout – Mogul skiing delivers the most demanding workout you can get while skiing downhill. When you dress for mogul skiing, therefore, remember that your body will generate more heat and perspiration than when you cruise groomed trails or run gates. I like to wear layers that I can easily unzip on the lift for a quick cool-down. I also prefer the newer, high-tech fabrics to cotton turtlenecks and thick wool sweaters.

11. HAVE FAITH, HAVE FUN

Now that you're familiar with mogul-skiing technique, you'll be surprised by the degree to which the skiers around you are unfamiliar with it. You'll meet instructors, racers and other groomed-trail experts who'll suggest that a narrow stance is, in all circumstances, outdated and incorrect, and that a more heavily steered turn is, in all circumstances, inferior to a purely carved or "arced" turn. Ignore them.

If you do most of your skiing at a racing-oriented area that has no freestyle program (most areas qualify), teaching your-self mogul technique could become a test of faith. You'll need to hold tightly to this book and ignore the inaccurate, mislead-ing suggestions you receive from the groomed-trail devotees around you. Bogus mogul-skiing advice runs rampant at racing-oriented areas, where groomed-trail experts tend to assume that their expertise extends beyond groomed trails.

The techniques I've described in this book are authentic, so don't let anyone draw you away from them. And let me give you a little history to embolden you on your mogul-skiing jour-ney. Mogul skiing grew out of the hot-dogging of the '60s and '70s. Despite its current World-Cup and Olympic status, the sport hasn't wandered completely away from its radical roots. It still requires of its practitioners a bit of rebelliousness. There is still a stodgy, groomed-trail mainstream that likes to suggest that the bumper's way is not the right way. So bumpers must occasionally go their own way and ignore the mainstream in order to understand and execute mogul technique.

As you move along the bump skier's path, know that you're not alone. Every bump skier has been frustrated, at one point or another, by the fact that mogul-skiing skills don't earn the wholehearted respect or recognition of the American skiing mainstream. The American skiing mainstream most often views great mogul skiers as impressive, but slightly freakish, risk-takers, rather than the skilled, poised, technically-minded, all-mountain experts they actually are.

If you have faith in what this book has taught you, and if you practice diligently, there'll soon come a day when you find it all working right. "This is what the bump skiers do!" you'll tell yourself as you zip smoothly down the fall line, absorbing and extending, steering your skis left and right, and eating up every bump and trough in your path. You'll realize then that you, too, have become a bump skier. And it won't matter to you that someone from the local ski school or racing club takes issue with your techniques or your "tactics," because you'll be having too much fun out-skiing most of the instructors and racers who venture into the bumps with you. And fun is, after all, what our sliding downhill on skis is all about.

GLOSSARY OF TERMS

Absorption and extension – the skier's absorption of the mogul, and the extension of the skier's legs as she passes through or over the trough.

Air – 1) A jump. 2) A jumping maneuver.

Air bump – A mogul that a skier uses as a jump.

Fall line – The path that a rolling ball would take down a ski slope, were that ball's direction not disrupted by moguls or other irregularities in the snow.

Flat spot – A mogul-less patch of snow that sits amidst moguls.

Flats – Mogul-less, groomed terrain.

Groomer – 1) A grooming machine. 2) The operator of that machine. 3) A mogul-less, groomed trail.

Hero bumps – a forgiving mogul field that allows for fast skiing and dramatic aerial maneuvers (soft snow, not too steep a trail, rhythmic bumps).

Home posture / home position – The tall, upright posture with which a mogul skier begins his run, and to which the mogul skier immediately returns after absorbing each mogul.

Landing bump – A mogul that a skier uses as a landing spot after a jump.

Lip – the very top of a jump or air bump.

Mogul line / line – the path upon which the skier directs her skis as she moves her torso straight down the fall line of a mogul trail.

Mogul skiing – to move one's torso straight down the mogul trail's fall line while the legs absorb the bumps, extend into the troughs, and turn the skis.

Pop — to push yourself skyward as you leave the lip of a jump or air bump.

Rotary-powered turn — the style of turn used by mogul skiers; a turn characterized by more rotary / twisting motion than most groomed-trail devotees tend to use.

Rotary motion — Twisting / steering motion that turns the skis.

Separation — the separation of upper-body motion (torso, arms, head) and lower-body motion (legs). In mogul sking, "good separation" means that the upper body descends the hill without abrupt or flailing absorption movements, while the legs pump rapidly up and down through the bumps, doing all of the absorption-and-extension work. (Among groomed-trail experts, "separation" usually refers to upper-body counter-rotation, rather than absorption and extension.)

Steer — to turn the skis with rotary / twisting force.

Touch — the subtle adjustment of absorption and extension that allows the bump skier to maintain both speed and control.

Trough — the low ravine that sits between moguls.

Trough hopping — a technique that allows the mogul skier to hop from one bump to the next, or from a flat spot to a bump. Mogul skiers use trough hopping to avoid bad snow conditions and to navigate irregular moguls.

Twin tips — 1) turned up ski tails, a feature on some of today's mogul skis (and all terrain-park skis); 2) skis that have twin tips.

Zipper line — the zipper-shaped path along which one's skis travel during mogul skiing.

Printed in the United States
97352LV00004B/188/A

9 781420 861594